Unleashing the Social Butterfly Within

The Ultimate Guide to building connections and making friends

KERRY HARDING

PREFACE

Even since I was young I remember being a terribly shy kid. In kindergarten I would always spend the whole day alone and even until college I would just have a small group of three or four friends (all of my same sex because I was terrified of people of the opposite sex) and was always known as the quiet and shy guy in the room.

I even started seeing a psychiatrist at some point during college. He prescribed antidepressants, which became a band aid fix. My anxiety and confidence levels were dependent on them.

I obviously got much better and sociable at the time, but when I eventually stopped taking these medications I felt anxious and insecure. I never had any therapy so without my chemical crutch I was afraid I would not be able to be more open and confident.

I spent a couple of years like that, I had proven to myself that I could be more open and outspoken and that it was not hard, but I was not sure if I would be able to do it without any drugs.

So I started meeting people online. I started striking conversations with people from the same city and neighborhood. Little by little I started to discover that, while not everyone would like me, I could be a very likeable and friendly person. One day I decided to meet in real life one of the persons I met online, she was a girl and, as I said, I had always been terribly afraid of the opposite sex.

It was awkward at first and even she asked me if I was nervous, but at some point I remember I had done this before and reassured myself I could do it again, with or without drugs or any other kind of external help. And things went much better after that. I made her laugh and we both had a great time. She wanted to see me again and she even talked about me to her friends.

As soon as I got to my home a very strong feeling of amazement sank upon me; I had been afraid of that my whole life? It was relatively easy! It was a little bit tricky at the beginning but as soon as I got past that initial part, it had become so much easier!

The same usually applies for many of the things in life we are afraid of: these new challenges seem much more difficult than they really are. We create these huge and monstrous fears in our heads and when we finally face them, we realize they were not that huge or hard to begin with; we just had created this complex web of insecurities and fears and had refused to see past them. But as soon as we touch them, they collapse, and we realize how small and simple these challenges really were and that those fears were mostly mirages: the expectations were much bigger than the challenge itself.

I don't want you to spend your whole life being afraid or insecure about social interactions, about meeting new people, about getting them to like you, to persuade and charm them; I don't want anyone to spend a whole life being afraid of that before deciding to face that fear (something which people sometimes never do); so I wrote this guide to help you save all that effort, suffering and work; so you can quickly learn how to do what it took me virtually a lifetime.

CONTENTS

INTRODUCTION

The social part of human life is the single most important and relevant part of any person, and this also applies for any other single living organism too. Think about it for a minute: the whole purpose of any biological species is to be successful and ensure it will continue to exist on this planet, perpetuating itself and its members; as such, it is only natural that the most of our lives revolve directly or indirectly about our social life, and when you do not perform well on that aspect, then you simply do not feel ok, if you do, you can feel 'incomplete'.

Your interpersonal universe is everything. The way people look at you has a great impact on you, it can bring you down or it can elevate you, and keeping that image is a hard full-time job.

The purpose of this book is to help readers to understand the importance of having a well-developed and healthy social life. The second thing we want you to achieve is not only to show you how to develop that, but to develop your social skills as much as it is possible for you.

HOW TO USE THIS GUIDE

As explained above, this guide's approach covers all the areas of a person's life as a whole: their relationships, the psychological approaches and their mental health, among others. We will cover each area in their own unique and separate chapters, at the end you will find a list of important notes taken from the preceding chapter which you should remember and observe always (taking notes is advisable). That is your List of Essentials.

After the List of Essentials you will find a series of simple exercises related to the preceding chapter, which you should perform and complete to reinforce what you just learned.

Be ready and pay attention! Remember also to be perceptive and open to new suggestions and lessons; and, finally, use your own common sense to identify those lessons that you need to apply to your life and figure out how to best apply them to your own unique situation: use your head, make the necessary efforts and be consistent.

Good luck!

IMPORTANT IDEAS AND ESSENTIAL CONCEPTS

First things first, you need to understand the essential concepts we will work in.

What do we mean with the "social component of your life"? We mean your entire social universe: all those areas of your life you share and spend with others, including any kind of interpersonal relationship, with your family, friends and your significant other (we will use this to refer to your boyfriend, girlfriend or any other sexual partner towards whom you have romantic feelings which are reciprocated and with whom you have established a formal and consistent relationship).

To preserve those relationships and that entire personal world of yours and to form and establish new ones you make use of your personal skills. Everyone has them, you may have strong and well-developed social skills or poor ones, but you have them, just as anybody else; even people with autism (we will talk more about this and other clinical conditions later on) has social skills, just that they do not possess strong ones or do not make much use of them, choosing sometimes not to invest time in their social universe.

Social skills are learnt through a process known as socialization and this process takes part during childhood and adolescence, up to the early adulthood. But even after this process ends you can still develop and acquire new social skills or to improve the ones you already have.

SOCIAL SKILLS

As we saw above, your social skills are the abilities you posses with which you establish, develop and maintain relationships with other people.

Everyone has got them, maybe they are not very well-developed, but they are there; you just need to find them and strengthen them if you need.

Let's work now with your social skills, in this chapter we will identify and strengthen them.

Empathy

First of all, what is Empathy? You may or may not know but, regardless, let's see the correct definition of this concept. Empathy Is the skill or capacity one person has that allows him or her to understand the ot her person, to see things from their point of view. In more simple terms, we can say that empathy is the art of being able to get yourself in someone else's shoes.

So, empathy is essential for the development of any relationship or to maintain those you already have.

Empathy should allow you not just to see a situation through the eyes of others, but to share their feelings, to feel happy with and for them, to feel sad with and for them.

Every person has empathy, to different degrees, you only have to develop. Everyone has empathy for we are genetically programmed to belong to and care for our peers, for our entire species.

The word "Empathy" is derived from the Greek word 'empatheia'.

It is composed of two Ancient Greek words: 'en' which means "at" or "in" and 'pathos' which means "suffering" or "passion".

So it can be read as: "to be in or at someone else's suffering".

Exercise:

To develop your empathy you have to practice and use your imagination and creativity.

Let's assume that someone close to you lost a loved one and is suffering. In this sad case you will have to create a realistic scenario in your head: how would you feel if you lost someone you love just as your friend? Picture yourself in that sad situation, include every detail in your scenario, others crying and suffering and you thinking how you would never be able to see that person again, to never be with him or her, ever again.

Now you get the idea and you can apply this occasionally in any other situation; after a while, you will start to feel their emotions and feel the way they do, automatically.

Add to your List of Essentials!

✓ Be coherent: this is a no-brainer: if someone who is close to you is suffering you will not act happy even if you are; but that is an extreme example, in more subtle situations you have to be coherent: for example, if someone close to you feels happy because he or she bought clothes they like but you do not, then you obviously will not criticize them outright, you will make a simple compliment and then forget about it, or you can talk to them and make a suggestion and respectfully express your opinion.

✓ Remember what we saw above: someone's freedom ends where yours start.

Tolerance

Tolerance and patience are other very essential components that you should always apply not only to the people who are close to you, but everywhere in this society.

The idea is simple: respect others, no matter how much you do not like their ideas, looks or activities; you respect and tolerate and you will be respected and tolerated back.

Tolerance and respect, however, have a limit: the freedom of someone ends where your own freedom starts. For example, someone smokes and you hate that, but you will tolerate it, or if he or she is close to you, you might make a (respectful) comment to them about the benefits of quitting smoking. So you respect, but what if the other person starts smoking inside your home? You would then have every right to confront them, even kicking them out; tolerance and patience are ALWAYS necessary, but they also have a limit which everyone should respect, including you; for example (a random example), you are a guy who likes to wear kilts and even skirts; no one has a right to tell you anything, and no one will, but what would happen if you go out naked? Someone will demand you to get dressed, as it is offensive.

Exercise

To develop your empathy you have to practice and use your imagination and creativity.

Let's assume that someone close to you lost a loved one and is suffering. In this sad case you will have to create a realistic scenario in your head: how would you feel if you lost someone you love just as your friend? Picture yourself in that sad situation, include every detail in your scenario, others crying and suffering and you thinking how you would never be able to see that person again, to never be with him or her, ever again.

Now you get the idea and you can apply this occasionally in any other situation; after a while, you will start to feel their emotions and feel the way they do, automatically.

Persuasion

Being convincing and persuasive is one of the strongest and most important social skills you can have or develop. I don't even have to explain you the reason, being able to convince others of sharing your point of view, ideas and beliefs, or to help you work with you is always in your best interest.

There is no universal strategy for being able to persuade others about something in particular and there are many ways to influence others; for example, if you are a 3-year old then simply screaming or crying might suffice to get others to do or to give you what you want, if you are a with someone that is physically attracted to you then flirting is an option or if you are with a subordinate then giving an order is all you need to do.

However, as you can see, in all these cases there is something that doesn't feel quite right, and it is that in these scenarios the person being "persuaded" was either being coerced or sort of "bribed", and to be truly effective and successful at persuading someone you will need to follow five simple principles which will make it more likely for you to persuade the other party.

1. To persuade someone the first thing you will need is to understand what they need and what they want. When proposing an idea or a plan you need to emphasize the benefits, the general benefits and, most importantly, the benefits that are relevant to whoever is you are trying to persuade. To be able to do this you will obviously need to know the other person very well and to have worked with your empathy.

2. The second thing you will need is to keep in mind that people do not really like sudden and big changes, even an impulsive person who likes new adventures likes to preserve a good degree of consistency and monotony in their lives, in their feelings and in their beliefs. So, for example, if you want to go out with a girl you like but she hasn't dated anyone in a long time and is hesitant, then invite her to see a movie she has been expecting for some time or to a concert of her favorite band, that way she will not feel she's not being taken off her normal routine.

3. The third thing is to get them to like you as much as possible. If you are trying to persuade a good friend then that would not really be much of a problem but if you are dealing with people you do not know very well then starting the conversation by talking about

things in common is a good idea: if they like sports then talk about last night's game, if they like to cook then ask them about a recipe, etc.

4. The fourth is to earn their trust. They will have to know you can be trusted and the best way to get them to trust you is for you to trust them first and to trust them openly. How? Just be honest with them and share some inside information with them, that way they will realize you consider them trustworthy and that you like them. For example, if you are at college, your homework is incomplete and would like someone you do not very well to let you copy theirs you can say something like: "Look, I'll be honest with you, I had to study for this other exam and by 2 am I had fallen asleep without even noticing".

5. The fifth and final thing is to let the other person you are trying to persuade that he or she is not alone. For example, if you want someone within a group to sign a petition then he or she will be more likely to sign if you tell him or her that almost everyone else within that same group has already signed or agreed.

Add to your List of Essentials!

✓ When trying to get to know what the other person wants or needs remember never to be afraid of asking what is that they want, what are they looking for and what it would take for them to accept the idea or plan you are proposing to them.

✓ Whatever their particular and personal needs and wants are remember that every person shares the same basic wants and needs: we all want to be complimented, to be appreciated, to feel important, to be successful, to be loved, etc.

✓ When you are trying to persuade someone and remark how everyone else has agreed with you remember to tell them about others who are *similar* to them. For example, if you want your neighbor to agree to a collective proposal then you will have to tell him how almost everyone in the neighborhood has agreed, but if you tell him that proposal has been widely supported in another city he may not care.

Being a good listener

By definition, a conversation involves an exchange of information between two parties: two or more parties talking to each other, so being able to effectively communicate your ideas or to persuade someone is only a half of the process; you also need to be a good listener and to make the other person you are talking to that he or she is being listened and that you give them attention they deserve.

This is as important as being able to make them listen clearly and seriously consider what you say or to convince them of what you have to say.

There are two important things you will need to figure out about what the other person who is talking to you and this will be helpful if you are having a hard time trying to understand them; just answer these two questions:

Why are they talking to you?

What are they trying to tell you?

If you cannot answer those two questions with what they are telling you then do not be afraid to ask them more questions or to interrupt them and ask them to explain something more in-depth.

Exercise

One of the hardest parts for someone with poorer social skills is to express their emotions and thoughts; so naturally, they might find it difficult to make facial expression and always seem to have a thoughtful or serious face.

If whenever you engage other person (not just when you are listening to what they say) you find it difficult to make facial expression then practice in front of a mirror: smile for five minutes, make a serious expression for another five and finally try to look sad for another five minutes.

This way if the other person says something funny you could laugh or simply smile as a courtesy (even if you are not particularly amused by what they say and this way they will find you more likeable too), adopt a serious expression if the subject at hand is serious, wince or look worried if they are telling you about a problem they had or make whatever appropriate facial expression as needed.

Add to your <u>List of Essentials</u>!

- ✓ Always pay attention, if you truly are not interested at all in what the other person is saying then send them away or tell them outright that you simply are not interested in what they are saying.
- ✓ If you do are interested then focus, pay attention to the other person. If you mind tends to wander away then pay attention to their words and fix your eyes in theirs or in their mouth.
- ✓ If what the other person wants to tell you or what you two want to talk about is important then you might want to limit the number of distractions: ask them to discuss that issue in private, ask them to step into your house or invite them a coffee; go to a more private environment where you can discuss the subject with fewer distractions.
- ✓ Remind them often that you are listening to what they say; paying attention to what they say is obviously the most important part, but letting them know you are paying attention might sometimes be just as important. To do this you might nod when they make an affirmation or make short and brief comments such as: "Sure", "I understand", "Of course", "You are right", or something like that. In short, engage them and make yourself an active part of the conversation.

Face rejection

There is an old saying in the Spanish-speaking world: "we are not all made of gold", which means that you are not perfect and certainly not everyone will like you.

Be prepared to face rejection from others, if you are ignored or brushed off by someone you just said hi to, then forget about, it does not matter; if you are trying to meet someone you are interested in (for any reason) and they turn you down or reject you, then try again sometime later. Think about what you might have done wrong and find out what they like so you can start a new conversation that will be more interesting to them.

However, you might not always be accepted by everyone and you are not perfect or have universal tastes and things in common with every single person in the world; so be prepared to be not like by everyone. This is normal and you will just have to accept it as a fact of life and move on.

Learn when and how to ignore

Just as you are going to be rejected or ignored sometimes, you will also have to learn to reject those that are not of interest to you or those who you do not consider as useful, productive and positive relationships.

You do not need to have rude or brusque to them to send them away (although this might be just what you will have to do if they persist in seeking you out). If they want to start a conversation with you, then you might excuse yourself or tell them you are busy with a smile and go away.

Exercise

Identify who you want to ignore, you can make a list (written in paper or in your head) about those persons you do not have an interest in talking to or having any sort of interaction or relationship to. They might be people who seem like a bad influence, those you would prefer to stay away from; or simply those who you do not like at a personal level, for any reason.

Add to your <u>list of essentials</u>!

- ✓ Do not be afraid to ignore someone you do not like or even to be more forceful or rude if they insist in trying to talk to you or see you.

Valuable retribution

This is very important: in a relation, in any relation you have to offer something to the other person. It may sound callous but it is always true and any relationship has to beneficial for both parties, so that the other person has to find something valuable in you; it could be that you make them happy, make them laugh, or you teach them things they do not know but they need to see a benefit, if they do not then they will lose interest in that relationship and even forget about you altogether; people usually do this subconsciously, it is not something that they plan, and some people might even react with aversion to this idea at first.

However, you have to be objective and decide whether or not the relationships in your life

OBSTACLES TO A HEALTHY SOCIAL LIFE

Certain things can impede or impair your ability to develop or maintain a social presence and to keep a healthy social life. Depending on the cause, these can be serious or simple things that can be dealt with easily.

Anxiety

Every person feels nervousness and feels anxiety because of different situations in their lives.

Anxiety is a normal emotion and a normal response to many situations, especially new ones and ones which involve the seeking of approval from others, be it a conscious or a subconscious search for approval.

However, as with any emotion, anxiety is a temporary situation and a temporary feeling. You can't feel happy forever or be sad forever, and you can't and will not feel anxious or nervous forever.

When you talk to a girl or a guy you feel attracted to, you are seeking his or her approval, and, again, you might do this consciously or subconsciously. When you are talking to someone you do not know very well or someone who you just met then, again, you are seeking their approval.

This is fine and is a normal situation, everyone needs somebody else's approval, we are social animals after all, we are not biologically programmed to live or be always alone or on our own and we are in fact so sociable that we domesticated other animals such as dogs or cats which we keep as pets and companions.

What is not normal is to let that seek for approval rule your entire life. You can't and should not get depressed or excessively nervous if the person you feel attracted to will not pay attention to you. You might feel a little bad but you will move on and forget about him or her. If you meet someone who does not likes you then you should not and will not feel depressed or start thinking too much about it; you just acknowledge the fact that person does not like you and you avoid him or her.

But in the end, the root and the cause for this anxiety is the natural need for approval we seek.

So, if you feel nervous when around people you do not know or people who you barely know or people from whom you seek approval then that is completely normal, and that phase is going to last less and less as you learn how to treat people. As you learn to accept yourself as you are despite others' disapproval then you this initial phase of nervousness will get smaller and smaller.

Clinical Conditions

A number of clinical conditions can affect the way we establish and develop new relationships, making it more difficult or much easier, depending on the case.

Certain diseases may almost completely abolish all social behavior and even all external displays of emotions (such as catatonia, although this is much rarer and a serious medical condition), so they can impair your social skills and your social development, sometimes even from a young age. Some diseases cause this by blunting the emotions of the individual, so they feel less interest in any interpersonal interaction, while others create distress in the individual in social situations and so make the person avoid those situations and create an active aversion towards social relationships.

If you feel your levels of anxiety are too high that they impair your daily life or find that you have absolutely no interest in establishing social relations, then you might consider making an appointment with your doctor so he can decide whether or not you have some clinical condition and treat it accordingly.

All and every disease requires professional medical assistance and treatment, and consultation with a psychologist if deemed necessary by the physician;

because it is as simple as this: any disease needs to be treated, so a more detailed explanation in this topic goes beyond the scope of this book, but we can be a brief overview of some of the most important and frequent diseases that affect our social performance nonetheless.

- Anxiety disorders
  Social anxiety disorder, Selective mutism
- Personality disorders
  Antisocial personality disorder, Avoidant personality disorder
- Pervasive developmental disorders
  Autism, Asperger syndrome, Rett syndrome, Childhood disintegrative disorder, High-functioning autism, among other forms of autism
- Schizophrenic disorders
  Schizoid, Schizotypical, Schizophrenia

On the other hand, a certain number of diseases such as Bipolar disease (during the manic phase) or Substance abuse disorders can make you hypersocial and make you feel or act inappropriately during social situations, with little regard for social conventions and norms. These diseases need also to be treated accordingly.

Remember, for a disease to qualify as such it needs to cause distress and/or impair the daily life of the subject, which is why homosexuality is not considered a disease.

So, if you feel any distress or discomfort in social situations or any other significant impairment in a persistent pattern (more than just 4 weeks) then making an appointment with a doctor is mandatory to rule out any condition and associated health ailments.

Finding people like you

If you try to meet and socialize with people with whom you share nothing in common and try to seek their approval then of course you will always feel nervous. It is ok to meet and get to know people who is different from you but don't even pretend to become close to them.

You should seek people who share many things in common with you, or who share just a few things in common with you, but that these things are important.

Find your own group and find several groups. You are a big fan of classical music? Then you should try making new friends with people who also like classical music as much as you do, but does this means you will only socialize with people who like classical music? No. You will have a group of friends who share that particular passion in common with you but you will also set different groups of people who share other things in common with you. The people who share the most in common with you will likely become your closer friends and probably even your some of your best friends.

Exercise

Identify which groups of persons that compose your social universe you might belong to and what things in common you share with the people in each of those groups. It is not necessary for those friends to know each other, just friends that are connected to you through your personal tastes and common shared interests.

You can even create a small diagram with circles, you being in the middle connecting to bigger circles, these bigger circles would represent the groups of people and inside you can include individual persons, whom in turn might be connected to other circles.

Add to your List of Essentials!

✓ Remember: you are not perfect, nobody is, but you can identify your defects and work on them, to be a better person. If you feel disapproval from others then that is normal, not everyone is going to like you, think what is it that the other person did not like about you, acknowledge it, change it if you think you can, but if you don't then forget about it and move on.

If you meet someone who practices a different religion and tries to avoid you or bothers you because of that, would you change your religion to please him or her? Of course not! If the reason for their disapproval is not something you want or are willing to change or work on, then forget about that person altogether and find someone who shares more in common with you.

UNSPOKEN COMMUNICATION: BODY LANGUAGE

The unspoken part of a dialogue is usually as important as the words the other person says; with the way I move my hands or set my posture others can usually tell some complex and important details such as whether I am angry or happy; and paying attention to what others are telling me or distracted; and essential stuff such as who am I addressing while talking.

The body language can also provide a strong emphasis to what I am trying to communicate to others; for example, if I close my fist when I say a word (and depending on the context) people will sense me as being determined to do or achieve what I am saying.

Why it is important?

What you do physically with your body while you speak is often as important as what you are actually saying to others and it is often more revealing too.

If the person who is talking to you is nervous enough you will most likely be able to tell right away: moving his arms all over the place, changing postures very often, appears not to know what to do with his hands or where to place them, supports his weight in one leg or the other intermittently, and in general simply does not stays still, the person seems restless and is all over the place.

And what if that same person is trying to sell you an idea, trying to convince you of the benefits, the advantages and the potential winnings of participating of or supporting his or her idea, all while being clearly and evidently nervous and appearing insecure; would you believe in what he or she is saying? Would you support them?

As much as a 93% of all the information you exchange with other people in your daily life is communicated through nonverbal means.

So, as you can see, the way you use your body and the postures you acquire are extremely important in relation to the message you are trying to convey to you listener. This whole system of nonverbal communication that usually happens along regular spoken communication is known as body language.

As we just saw in the first example above, body language is important mostly for two reasons: it is revealing towards the listener and for the impression it has the potential to cause in the listener.

Body language is revealing because whoever you are talking to can and will usually perceive how you really feel while you are talking, most of the times they do it subconsciously and automatically, if you are nervous, excited about whatever it is you are talking about, afraid, desperate or sad, people will usually be able to notice this and they will contrast it with your message and this will have very important consequences on their attitude towards you and their final opinions about what you are saying.

Body language is also important regarding the impression you may leave upon the listener because your nonverbal communication has the potential to immensely strengthen whatever you are saying. In fact, there is strong scientific evidence and recent research to indicate that whenever you interact with another person most of the information that you transmit (and that they transmit to you) is exchanged through nonverbal means; this means that any conversation (which is an exchange of information between two or more persons) most of the information exchanged is not transmitted speaking (Mehrabian, 1981).

Important common body postures

Most postures are not interpreted directly; for example, crossing your arms above your chest tends to portray insecurity but when you see someone doing it you might not think much of it. However, subconsciously, you are interpreting it and may change your attitude towards the person you are talking to. In this example, if you see someone crossing their arms, you might feel their insecurity and become more aggressive (if you do not like the other person or are confronting them or discussing something with them) to take advantage of their insecurity, or if you are not trying to confront them in any way then you might take a more conciliatory posture or lower your voice so as to make them feel better.

Among the postures that you should take note of are the following:

Clenching hands. Clenching hands is most usually used when the person who does it is trying to show they feel confident and in control, but in fact it tends to be a demonstration of feeling insecure or frustrated, even that the person in question is losing control and is trying desperately to show confidence. In general, it tends to be interpreted negatively and as a sign of anxiety. It is also used by people that do not know exactly what they are talking about but are trying to show expertise or an extensive knowledge on the subject, when in fact they do not have either. In this case, a clear example would be when a politician is asked a tough question during a debate or press conference and clenches his or her hands.

Crossing your arms. This one of the most common and carries a message of insecurity; when you cross your arms you do it to assume a defensive position and to cover your chest and put a distance or barrier between you and whoever you are talking to. It is also usually interpreted as a sign of boredom of lack of interest in what you are listening.

Hands behind your back. The exact opposite of crossing your arms above your chest is to hold your hands behind your back, this way you expose your chest and let the others know you are not afraid of them, that you feel confident and do not expect any sort of aggression. It might also show superiority and fearlessness. Think about it: we usually tend to imagine respected people or people with authority walking around with their hands behind their backs; priests, military officers, principals, etc.

Head over hand. Using your hand to completely support your head is a clear sign of boredom and disinterest. Sometimes a person can hold their heads above just a couple of fingers or the thumb, or they can completely let their heads rest entirely over the palm of their hands, which a more extreme and direct sign of boredom.

Hand on chin. This is very different than using your hands to support your head; here you use your hand to rub or hold your chin, that grasp can extend to a whole cheek or you can hold your chin and extend a finger upwards. This posture denotes interest in what you are hearing, it demonstrates that you are seriously and genuinely considering and analyzing what you are hearing, and/or that you are very interested on it.

Hands on waist. This one is when you put your hands in your waist, resting your arms in your hips and resulting in your arms bent almost at a 45° angle. The way you expose your arms makes you look bigger and makes you stand out, makes you getting noticed, while at the same time exposing your chest which has the same meaning as with the hands on back posture: you are exposing your vital organs because you are not afraid of who you are talking too, in fact you want to look bigger and stronger because you are ready for a confrontation, you expect a confrontation and perhaps you even want one; so this posture may transmit anger.

But depending on the context of the conversation this posture will not necessarily be interpreted as aggressive or belligerent, it can simply be meant as a way of showing a lot of self confidence or simply display readiness, that you are ready for action; for example, if in a formal conversation your boss is instructing you to do something and you assume this posture while listening to the details of the task, it will show him you are ready and eager to do what you are being told to do.

Various fidgets. There is a wide range of small and very subtle actions someone can do while listening to others such as playing with hair, playing with the ring on a finger, fiddling with whatever that person is holding in their hands at the moment, and many more. They all tend to seem completely unrelated to the situation and often they are and mean nothing. At most, they might mean that the person that does it has a anxious personality; maybe not much, maybe he or she likes to stay active. However, if they fidget around while looking down or actively avoiding looking at you, then that may mean two things: if they look down or avoid looking at you *while they talk*, then that might indicate they are either hiding something (perhaps related to what they are talking about) or feel nervous for talking about whatever they are talking about. If they fidget around and avoid looking at you directly or look down and *they are not talking* (just listening), then that means you make them nervous or intimidate them: maybe they feel intimidated because they are receiving a reprimand, maybe they feel physically attracted or repulsed by you, maybe they have something to hide from you and that makes them feel nervous, or maybe they are simply anxious person with not very good social skills.

Exercise

Take a few minutes and relax. Then try to remember a normal conversation you had with anyone else or your most recent interaction, one you can remember very well and very clearly.

Reenact that conversation or interaction in your head and try to remember how you handled the nonverbal part of that interaction, think about your body language.

Now identify which of the postures we saw above you used the most and take note of that.

Finally, ask yourself the following question: the postures you used the most conveyed insecurity, lack of self esteem, nervousness, desperation or any other unwanted feeling? If you did then you will now have to start working on that, if you find it difficult at first then you can start by doing nothing with your hands but without acquiring an unwanted body posture. A good posture you can use in which you do not need to use your hands but will not transmit any negative feeling is the one where you hold your hands behind your back, which (as we already saw above) will transmit self confidence and that you are in control of the situation.

Another positive posture in which you would not need to use your hands would be to assume the posture of putting your hands in your hips, but if you do this just remember it might be interpreted by your listener as belligerence depending on the context of the conversation (like if the conversation does not have a friendly tone).

However, as soon as you feel more comfortable you must remember to start using your arms, hands and your whole body to display positive postures and most importantly: be confident of yourself!

Add to your <u>List of Essentials</u>!

- ✓ Always look up! Do not keep your eyes on the ground or keep your stare lost.
- ✓ Walk and stand in public as if you have a right to be there, be confident and act confident.
- ✓ Never start fidgeting when others are talking to you, even if you are not really interested, just pretend you are, as a courtesy and avoid fidgeting.

ESTABLISHING INTERPERSONAL RELATIONSHIPS

Now it is time to work! Here, I will guide to the process of actually establishing new relationships and developing and strengthening those you already have.

Here will apply all you have learned from the previous reading; you can go back and check your notes (if you made any) or read again whatever you need; do not worry if you do not feel confident or seem very successful in the beginning, remember this is a long and arduous process and you may feel a bit discouraged at first, but if you make and consistent and honest effort, you will succeed in no time; so let's begin.

Making new friends

First thing you need to know this: you might be afraid of talking to new people, to people you don't know. **Don't be.**

You may at first think this will be a complex and long process, but as we saw above, it is nothing like that, and in fact, making new friends or developing friendships you already have is really simple and quick.

First of all remember the first and most important rule: you are not perfect, you will fail to get along with many and perhaps most people. This is because everyone is unique, and not everyone will have the same ideas, tastes or precepts that you have, so forget about being loved by everyone, forget about being able to come in and impress everyone; that is a myth and is not possible to achieve. Even if you could make everyone like you, you may not like them back.

This rule will have another important consequence you will have to keep in mind: you will fail to establish a rapport and develop a good personal relationship with many (in fact most) of the people you meet. You might keep a nice casual relationship limited to say hi and "have a good day", but a true, honest and personal friendship will be unlikely; a relationship like this is known as a casual or incidental relationship.

This brings us to the second rule: do not be afraid to discard and even ignore those persons with whom you do not have anything in common.

You do not even have to establish a casual relationship with everyone; which does not mean you have to pretend they do not exist or be rude: if you are forced to spend time with them (e.g. finding someone alone outside a classroom while waiting for the teacher to arrive, in which case you will be effectively forced to spend time with them), you can just make small talk, be nice to them and that's it.

Now, about establishing new meaningful relationships: you will first need to filter and forget about all those persons who do not interest you, those with whom you have nothing in common or you (or them) are not interested in developing a new and close friendship with.

As you might already imagine, the best way to know who are worth spending time with to develop a new friendship is to find those who you have the most in common with.

This is rather easy and you actually do not have to spend a lot of time thinking about it, as soon as you find the right person you will notice it immediately, you will feel comfortable around them, they will make you smile or laugh and they will start seeking your company too or sticking around when you talk to them, with them deciding you are worth it too and investing the necessary time out of their daily lives to establish a new friendship with you.

Once you find them then simply act naturally, do not force a conversation; make small talk the way you read about above while you find and identify the things you share in common with the other person you are talking with, this is establishing an effective initial rapport.

The most effective way to establish and consolidating an effective new friendship is to make the other person happy around you by making them laugh, giving them a fun time with you. But this is also the hardest thing to do. Actually, this is quite probably the hardest part you will have to learn to do in this guide. It is the hardest because of how much every person varies from the next one, there are no rules or basic instructions, just identify their tastes and say something funny, do not worry if they don't laugh or find what you say as funny, just brush it off and keep talking; this is hard because you will essentially have to learn how to do it on your own. However, once you start learning and gaining self confidence, you will find out that it is not hard at all, it is even fun.

Exercise

Strike a conversation with someone you don't know well. It does not has to be a complete stranger if you still feel uncomfortable about it, you can talk to someone who you see every day but have not spoken to yet; like a classmate, a coworker, the security guard who stands at the door of a building you go into every day, the guy who cuts your hair, or anyone.

Start small conversations at first, identify those you get along with the most and start to make longer conversations, identifying things you have in common.

By the end of a 10-day period you will have to have started conversations with at least two strangers.

Add to your List of Essentials!

- ✓ People you meet for the first time are usually as nervous as you, even if they don't show it externally.
- ✓ Do not be afraid of being rejected or ignored, remember: it is no big deal.

Preserving and consolidating existing relationships

Consolidating the relationships you already have or those you just made is a very different subject.

There are certain things and rules you will have to follow or observe to keep a relationship 'healthy' and here we will see them separately.

1. Trust
   This is widely considered the most important ingredient in any healthy relationship of any nature. If you do not feel like you can trust the other person in certain things or to allow him or her inside certain things or aspects of your life, then that might not be a relation as close as you might believe.

On the other hand, if you do trust them and they have earned your trust but they do not reciprocate by trusting you with certain things, then that might mean that even thought they are trustworthy and reliable people you consider your friends, they might not consider you their friend. You will have to reevaluate those relationships.

2. Communication

   This is related to the earlier point. For a relationship to be healthy both parts have to feel comfortable of telling each other anything they need to, either a personal thing (such as a problem they have) they need to talk about with someone else or a certain aspect of the relationship itself (such an issue they perceive between you two that they want to discuss).

   You and the other person in a relationship can't read each other's mind, if there is something they do not like about each other they will have to tell the other and talk it through.

3. Respect

   This is a very important aspect in any relationship. If you feel the other person in the relationship is using you, treats you poorly, ignores you, takes advantage of you in any way, leads you or takes you for granted, then talk to them, communicate as we saw in the earlier point. If that is not possible (for whatever reason) then you might consider ending that relationship; someone who appreciates you and truly cares about you will never take you for granted or treat you poorly in any way, shape or form, if they do, then they do not truly care about you or appreciate you. End that relationship.

4. Give them their space

   You will have to give the other person their own space to grow. Do not be all the time over them, do not try to manage all their issues and every small aspect of their lives and do not make their problems yours if they did not ask for your help about such problem. Give them their own space and their own time: you might have the closest relationship in the world but you still are two unique, separate and different people.

However, do not be distant and if you are truly worried about them or you feel something is wrong then trust them and ask them straight about that issue, if they need you they will let you know, if not, then let them be.

5. Humility

    This is very essential and the lack of this value usually ruins many good and healthy relationships, yet is very simple to understand and follow.

    Be humble. If you screw up or make a mistake, admit it both to yourself and to the other person, apologize if necessary, learn from it so you don't do it again and move on.

    Many times when we make a serious mistake that offends or hurts the other person inside a relationship; we might get into a fight and in the heat of the moment, end or seriously damage that relationship. Being humble will allow you to avoid that by simply being able to accept responsibility for your mistakes and actions.

Exercise

You might need to grab a pen or pencil and paper for this one. Just take a relation that is meaningful to you and analyze every single of the five key ingredients we just saw above; analyze and evaluate how are you performing on these aspects and then analyze how the other person is performing on those. You can even grade it from 1 to 5 if you want. Remember you have to be as objective as you can!

If a relationship you evaluate performs poorly when evaluated then it is time to evaluate and think whether that relationship is worth preserving at all; but if you treasure that friend or partner, then it might be worth a shot to try to fix things or improve on these aspects.

Add to your List of Essentials!

- ✓ When communicating to the other person in the relationship, remember to be honest, clear and straightforward; think beforehand what you want to talk about if you must.
- ✓ Always be as honest as you can and if you feel the other party is not being honest most of the time then you should consider ending that relationship because trust is one of the key ingredients to any relationship.
- ✓ Do not be blunt or take draconian measures; for example, if, inside one relationship, you or the other person fails in one or more of the key aspects we just reviewed, then it might be worth a shot to try to improve or fix things; you should only consider ending a relationship if other efforts fail.

GROUP CONVERSATION

Talking or being around big groups can be truly scary for someone who has little to no experience with this; and if you are reading this, changes are, you are your way to unleash your full potential within your social life.

Personally, my experience was a bit odd in that, during high school, talking to individual persons (especially pretty girls) used to freak me out, but if I had to go to the front of the classroom and speak I would feel less nervous, I would perform well. My teachers noted this and once told my parents that I was the quietest kid in the classroom but if asked to go to the front of the group, I would stand up and speak loud and clear.

The reason for this, according to my psychologist at the time, was that, in front of big groups I would obviously avoid the need to make eye contact; making eye contact makes the interaction more personal and when that is missing, I would make a group interaction something impersonal.

However, I could only talk about presentations that I prepared beforehand, saying things mechanically; I would never be able to talk about personal things or to inspire a group.

So, there are two things you need and want when it comes to talking to groups of people: to avoid anxiety and to be able to sway or influence their opinions.

Anxiety before large groups

To help ameliorate your anxiety before groups of people you should read and practice what we saw in the chapter "Obstacles to a healthy social life". The lessons and tips exposed there can be applied here except that it is easier to overcome the anxiety when speaking to groups of people than it is to talk to individual persons; even talking to large crowds might result even easier than talking to small groups. It is a strange rule: the larger the group of people, the easier it is to overcome your own anxiety.

The reason for this is that large groups of people tend to act by instinct, as a single entity, it is all part of group psychology. For example, during a fire inside a theater or enclosed area, everyone will follow the next guy: everyone will try to use the same emergency exit, even if there is another one a few meters apart. Investigations show individuals lose their personal identity and individuality, and adopt a group identity.

So, when talking to large groups, you are dealing not with a lot of individuals but with a single entity, a mass of people acting together.

Influencing or swaying the opinion of a group

This lesson will be rather simple and short, because, well, simply because it is.

You see, when people form groups and they fully integrate themselves into such groups, they tend to lose their individuality and their personal ideas and thoughts and act as a single entity, like a hive.

If, for example, a fire breaks out in a theater in which there are two or more emergency exits, everyone will try to escape through the same exit; every person will try to follow the closest person next to him or her, even if they do not know each other and everyone will run to the same part.

So, it is actually easier to convince, influence or to simply convey an idea to a group of people than to a single person. If you are before a large crowd of 50 or more people, and tell a joke then you only have to make 10 people laugh and the others will follow suit.

That is the key to influencing a large group of people: you just have to influence a larger percentage of the people in a crowd or group of people: you don't have to get all of them; you just have to get *most* of them. Of course, some individuals might not agree to what you are proposing, but it is unlikely they will express their contrary opinions in public; but this is an advantage for you: it will give you time to deal with them separately and individually.

So, in conclusion, it is much easier to deal with a large crowd than with a single one, in every aspect.

Exercises

1. Read again the Social Skills chapter, especially the part about Persuasion; remember that you have to use the same principles when convincing a group of people as when convincing a single

---

person. Now, ask yourself the following question: do you find it harder to speak in front of a crowd or a group of people? If you find it harder and yet it is easier then the difficulties lie within yourself only, your own anxiety and insecurities.

2. Also read again the chapter about Establishing interpersonal relationships, especially the *Making new friends* section. Why exactly? Well, as with single persons, you need to find and try to establish a relation with friendly crowds; it is better to talk, convince or sell an idea to a friendly crowd than to a group of people you have nothing in common with, and you will be more successful.

Add to your <u>List of Essentials</u>!

- ✓ When trying to influence or sell an idea to a group, you must remember to essentially follow the same rules and principles you use when you are trying to persuade someone, just as we saw earlier in the Social Skills chapter: identify their common needs and offer them what they want, as much as you can.
- ✓ Remember the recommendations we saw relating to meeting new people: do not be afraid of them, no one is better or superior to you in any aspect, no matter how many people they are, one, ten or a hundred, you should not be afraid of them.
- ✓ If you feel anxiety talking to or in front of a large group of people, just imagine you are talking with a single mass, to a hive; you can even imagine you are talking to a single person.
- ✓ Regarding eye contact, you do not have to establish direct eye contact with every single person in the group or crowd; you just have to look at one person at a time, briefly, just for 5 seconds at most, and then fix your gaze in another different person. Remember to cover everyone in the group, or, if the group is very large, then you will just have to mentally divide the crowd in four

sections, and to establish eye contact with one person of each section, thus covering the whole crowd.

FINAL RECOMMENDATIONS AND THOUGHTS

This guide has come to an end, and I would like us to have final look at the most important and common concepts we have learned and studied here.

- ✓ The first thing you need to fully develop your social skills and life is self-confidence; trust yourself, whatever you need to do, you CAN do it!

- ✓ The second is to be able to accept failure; you are not perfect, you will fail and you will sometimes be rejected by others, we all do, not everyone can like you or find you interesting; rejection and failure are a normal part of the human experience and they are no big deal at the end, just accept it and move on, like everybody else!

- ✓ Finally, have fun and have a good time! Meeting new people and being social should be a nice and fun experience, do not take it too seriously! Learning to develop your social skills is important but it should not be taken too seriously, it should (in a small part at least) come naturally and be an interesting and fun experience.

Good luck and have fun!

WANT MORE FROM KERRY HARDING?

Here is a preview of Confidence in Conversation..

Introduction

There are those among us who seem to take conversation and socializing for granted. There are those that seem to have little interest in such things. And then there are those of us that want to be able to speak, and socialize, and play, and interact with that natural confidence and ease but…try as they might, it just doesn't happen.

This can be extremely disheartening. It can lead to very low self-esteem, loneliness, frustration and a ton of other negative emotional states that people could really do without. But what if those people could find the secret to unlocking their inner conversation virtuoso and become the natural conversationalist they dream of being without having to fundamentally change anything about their character?

In truth, that previous sentence broadly sums up the solution; everyone has it within them to apply their character in a way that makes them a confident conversationalist. The trick is unlocking it; breaking through whatever barriers are preventing it from reaching the surface!

In this book, we will cover a comprehensive approach to explore yourself and discover the unique, fascinating individual that you are. Then, by working in a few all-purpose tricks and overlying principles for the practice of self-empowerment, we will help you through the process of applying yourself in conversation to eventually achieving the confidence and graceful ease that some people have in conversation.

The steps are not complex, but will be challenging. The process is not insurmountable, but will require you to take small steps outside of your comfort zone. The result, over time, will be that you amass a depth of positive experiences in conversation that gradually bolster your confidence, and provide you with the foundations you need to find your own way into a world of enjoyable, interesting and constructive conversations.

Open your mind, and read on…

Chapter 1 – The Importance of Body Language

As you may or may not know, a lot of communication is non-verbal. I might not tell you I feel upset with you, choosing instead to physically retreat from you; if you don't catch these non-verbal cues, you might not realize that something is wrong. Similarly, the body language you are communicating might make you seem unapproachable or awkward. Fortunately, with a little research, you can make body language a positive part of your social interactions.

When Your Body Language And Your Words Don't Agree

Awareness of one's own body language is something not many people consider. Even the most careful consideration of what words to use can be completely undermined by the accompanying non-verbal signals. When your words and your body are conveying different messages, people will often find the body language more telling. Accidentally sending the wrong message this way can cause trouble!

Here is a preview of How to Be Witty..

Chapter 1 - Understanding the Merits of

Being a Good Conversationalist

Have you ever found yourself enthralled by a witty conversationalist? Have you been in a situation where people are so rigid that you become too self-conscious yourself? Don't you sometimes wish you had the ability to enliven an otherwise bland and dull conversation?

Being witty actually presents a lot of uses, most of which are geared to make you a better conversationalist and be more adept at dealing with social situations. Here are a few of such uses:

Witticisms can serve as effective ice breakers. When people in a group are too caught up with rules and a striking fear of rejection, it can be very difficult to establish a connection. In these types of situations, sometimes all it takes is one perfectly concocted comeback to make everyone comfortable and allow them to let go of the notion that they are being judged.

Conversations with strangers can be hard, so attempts at establishing rapport with them are certainly welcome. Being witty is one of the ways you can build rapport.

Being witty can also serve as a flirting tool. When done right, it's the perfect way to catch anyone's attention without causing unnecessary tension and awkwardness.

Making witty remarks is a great way of acknowledging what others just said. It shows that you are an active listener and that you are actually paying attention to what other people are saying.

Being witty is a trait that you are not born with. Instead, it is something that can be achieved through dedication, commitment and a continuous desire to be better at handling conversations. If you feel you have what it takes to be witty, now is as good a time as any to nurture such potential.

On this note, the succeeding chapters provide a detailed discussion of who a witty conversationalist is and what it entails to be one.